BHARATANATYAM TO KATHAK

A JOURNEY THROUGH INDIA'S DANCE TRADITIONS

DR. JAGADEESH PILLAI

Made with ♥ on the Notion Press Platform
www.notionpress.com

|| "Dedicated to all who seek to understand and appreciate Indian culture and tradition." ||

ঌ

Contents

Contents

PRAYER

"Om Poornamadah Poornamidam Poornat Poornamudachyate,Poornasya Poornamaadaya Poornamevavashishyate,Om Shantih, Shantih, Shantih"

The literal interpretation of this mantra is: That which is Absolute, This which is Absolute, Absolute arises from Absolute, If Absolute is removed from Absolute, Absolute remains OM Peace, Peace, Peace.

About The Author

Dr. Jagadeesh Pillai is a renowned Guinness World Record holder, writer, and researcher hailing from Varanasi, also known as the abode of Lord Shiva. With a Ph.D. in Vedic Science and a range of creative ideas and achievements, he is a true polymath. He is the author of more than 100 books including Research Publications. Although his roots can be traced back to Kerala, the people of Varanasi hold him in high regard and affectionately consider him one of their own.

Dr. Pillai has achieved four Guinness World Records in the following subjects:

"Script to Screen" - In this record, Dr. Pillai produced and directed an animation film within the shortest time possible, breaking the previous record set by Canadians. He has also received numerous national and international awards and recognitions for this achievement.

Longest Line of Postcards - For this record, Dr. Pillai created a line of 16,300 postcards on the occasion of the 163rd anniversary of Indian Postal Day. The event also included a questionnaire about the Indian flag.

Largest Poster Awareness Campaign - Dr. Pillai designed an awareness campaign on the subject of "Beti Bachao - Beti Padhao" (Save the Girl Child - Educate the Girl Child) to achieve this record.

Largest Envelope - In tribute to the Indian Prime Minister's

"Make in India" initiative, Dr. Pillai created a 4000 square meter envelope using waste paper to achieve this record.

Attempted - **70000 Candles on a 210 kg Cake** - To celebrate the 70th Indian Independence Day, Dr. Pillai attempted to light 70,000 candles on a 210 kg cake, which was recorded in World Records India.

Attempted - **Documentary on Dhamek Stupa of Sarnath in 17 Languages** - Dr. Pillai attempted to create a documentary on the Dhamek Stupa of Sarnath, dubbing it in 17 different languages. The result of this attempt is currently awaiting confirmation from the Guinness World Records.

Dr. Pillai is skilled in teaching the Bhagavad Gita, a Hindu scripture, and is popular among young people. He has helped many young people improve their lives through his motivational teachings.

In addition to teaching, he has composed and sung numerous Sanskrit Bhajans and patriotic songs.

He has also written and directed several short films and documentaries for awareness campaigns, and has volunteered with the police in both UP and Kerala to spread awareness about various issues through videos and photography.

Incredibly, he has produced and directed over 100 documentaries about the city of Varanasi, all on his own.

He has also helped and guided more than 25 boys and girls to achieve world records through creative and innovative methods. He is a multifaceted person who uses his intellect and the blessings given to him by God to excel in various areas. He is both a teacher and a student, always learning and teaching, and is able to master any subject he comes across.

He is a selfless social activist and motivational speaker who has overcome struggles and failures to become a successful and enthusiastic individual with a rich life experience.

In addition to his work with the Bhagavad Gita, he is also an efficient Tarot card reader, Astro-Vastu consultant, and a talented singer and composer. He has sung the entire Ram Charita Manas and Bhagavad Gita in his own compositions, and has sung the phrase "Lokah Samastha Sukhino Bhavantu" in 50 different languages. He is currently working on a detailed and scientific study of Vedas, Upanishads, Puranas, and the Bhagavad Gita. He has also composed and sung the Hanuman Chalisa and Gayatri Mantra in 108 and 1008 different compositions, respectively.

Awards - Four Times Guinness World Records, Winner of Mahatma Gandhi Vishwa Shanti Puraskar, Mahatma Gandhi Global Peace Ambassador, Kashi Ratna Award, Dr. APJ Abdul Kalam Motivational Person of the Year 2017, Mother Teresa Award, Indira Gandhi Priyadarshini Award, Bharat Vikas Ratna Award, Udyog Ratna Award, Vigyan Prasar Award, Poorvanchal Ratn Samman.

PREFACE

The book "**Bharatanatyam to Kathak: A Journey Through India's Dance Traditions**" aims to delve into the rich and diverse world of Indian dance. It aims to provide an understanding of the different dance forms, their origins, cultural significance, and how they continue to be relevant in today's world.

The book begins with an introduction to Indian dance, providing a general overview of the different dance forms and their place in Indian culture. It then goes on to explore the classical dance forms of India, including Bharatanatyam, Kathak, Kathakali, Kuchipudi, Mohiniyattam, and Odissi. The book also delves into the folk dances of India and the religious and ritual dances, highlighting their unique characteristics and cultural significance.

The book also examines the impact of Indian classical dance on the modern world, exploring how it has influenced other dance forms and styles and its ability to promote cross-cultural understanding and appreciation. The book also explores the Bollywood and Indian pop dance, which are becoming increasingly popular around the world.

In addition, the book also covers the education and training of Indian dance, and the importance of conservation and preservation of these dance forms. The book concludes by highlighting the ongoing relevance and significance of Indian dance in today's world.

Overall, this book is an in-depth exploration of Indian dance and its cultural and spiritual significance. It is intended for anyone with an interest in Indian culture, dance, and the arts, and it aims to provide a deeper understanding and appreciation of the rich and diverse world of Indian dance.

I

Introduction: Understanding Indian Dance

Indian dance is a vibrant and diverse art form that has a rich history and cultural significance. It encompasses a wide range of styles, from classical forms such as Bharatanatyam and Kathak, to folk and tribal dances. Each dance form has its own unique characteristics and tells a different story.

One of the most important aspects of Indian dance is its spiritual connection. Many dance forms, particularly classical forms, are rooted in religious rituals and ceremonies. For example, Bharatanatyam, which originated in the southern state of Tamil Nadu, is heavily influenced by Hinduism and is often performed as an offering to the gods. Similarly, Kathak, which originated in the northern state of Uttar Pradesh, has strong connections to the Bhakti movement and is often performed as a form of devotion.

Another important aspect of Indian dance is its use of hand gestures, or mudras. These gestures convey different emotions and ideas, and are an essential part of the dance performance. For example, the "abhaya" mudra, in which the dancer raises their hand with the palm facing outwards, symbolizes fearlessness and protection.

Indian dance is also known for its intricate footwork and complex rhythms. The dancers use a variety of steps and movements to create a dynamic and fluid performance. Many classical dance forms also incorporate elements of acting and storytelling, making them a complete form of expression.

Folk and tribal dances are also an important part of the Indian dance tradition. These dances are typically performed by communities and often have a strong connection to the local culture and environment. For example, the Garba dance, which is popular in the state of Gujarat, is performed during the Navaratri festival and is associated with the worship of the goddess Durga.

In conclusion, Indian dance is a multi-faceted art form that has deep cultural and spiritual significance. It encompasses a wide range of styles, from classical forms to folk and tribal dances, each with its own unique characteristics and stories. The intricate hand gestures, footwork, and rhythms make it a dynamic and fluid performance, and the acting and storytelling elements make it a complete form of expression.

"Indian classical dance is a celebration of the body, mind, and spirit."

II

The Classical Dance Forms of India

Indian classical dance forms are a rich and diverse tradition that has been passed down through generations. These dances are characterized by their intricate movements, gestures, and rhythms, as well as their deep cultural and spiritual significance. Some of the most well-known classical dance forms of India include Bharatanatyam, Kathak, Kathakali, Kuchipudi, and Odissi.

Bharatanatyam is one of the oldest and most popular classical dance forms of India. It originated in the southern state of Tamil Nadu and is heavily influenced by Hinduism. The dance is characterized by its grace and fluidity, as well as its use of hand gestures, or mudras, to convey different emotions and ideas. Bharatanatyam is often performed as an offering to the gods and is considered to be one of the most sacred dance forms in India.

Kathak is another classical dance form that originated in northern India. It has its roots in the Bhakti movement and is characterized by its fast-paced footwork and intricate rhythms. Kathak dancers often tell stories through their actions, using gestures and facial expressions to convey different emotions and ideas.

Kathakali is a classical dance-drama form that originated in the southern state of Kerala. It is known for its elaborate costumes and makeup, as well as its use of hand gestures and facial expressions to convey different emotions and ideas. Kathakali performances typically last for several hours and often tell stories from Hindu mythology.

Kuchipudi is a classical dance form that originated in the southern state of Andhra Pradesh. Its fluid movements and elegant footwork characterize it. Kuchipudi performances often tell stories through dance, using gestures and facial expressions to convey different emotions and ideas.

Odissi is a classical dance form that originated in the eastern state of Odisha. It is characterized by its fluid movements and use of hand gestures, or mudras, to convey different emotions and ideas. Odissi performances often tell stories from Hindu mythology, such as the stories of Lord Krishna.

Indian classical dance forms are a rich and diverse tradition that has been passed down through generations. Each dance form has its own unique characteristics, such as Bharatanatyam's grace and fluidity, Kathak's fast-paced footwork and intricate rhythms, Kathakali's elaborate costumes and makeup, Kuchipudi's fluid movements and elegant footwork, and Odissi's fluid movements and use of hand gestures. These dance forms are also deeply rooted in the culture and spirituality of India, and often convey stories, emotions, and ideas through movements, gestures and rhythms.

"Through Indian dance, we connect with our heritage and preserve our cultural identity."

ဢ

III

Bharatanatyam

Bharatanatyam: The Dance of Tamil Nadu and connected with other parts of southindia

Bharatanatyam is a classical dance form that originated in the southern state of Tamil Nadu in India. It is one of the oldest and most popular classical dance forms in India and has a rich cultural and spiritual history. The dance is characterized by its grace and fluidity, as well as its use of hand gestures, or mudras, to convey different emotions and ideas.

Bharatanatyam is heavily influenced by Hinduism, and is often performed as an offering to the gods. The dance is rooted in the Natya Shastra, an ancient Indian treatise on the performing arts, and is believed to have been performed in temple dances as a form of worship. In addition, it is believed that the dance was originated by the Devadasis, the temple dancers, who were dedicated to the temple deity and were considered as a spiritual medium to connect with the divine.

The dance form is known for its intricate footwork and complex rhythms. Dancers use a variety of steps and movements to create a dynamic and fluid performance. Bharatanatyam also incorporates elements of acting and storytelling, making it a complete form of expression.

Bharatanatyam is not limited to Tamil Nadu alone, it is also popular in other parts of South India such as Andhra Pradesh, KarnATAKA, and Kerala. In Andhra Pradesh it is known as "Kuchipudi", in KarnATAKA it is known as "Yakshagana" and in Kerala it is known as "Mohiniyattam". Each of these dance forms have their own unique characteristics and styles, but they all share a common origin in the Natya Shastra and are considered to be part of the Bharatanatyam tradition.

In recent years, Bharatanatyam has gained popularity around the world, and is now performed by dancers of all backgrounds. It is considered as a powerful medium for self-expression and has been used to raise awareness about important social and political issues.

In conclusion, Bharatanatyam is a classical dance form that originated in the southern state of Tamil Nadu in India. It is characterized by its grace and fluidity, as well as its use of hand gestures, or mudras, to convey different emotions and ideas. The dance is deeply rooted in Hinduism and has a rich cultural and spiritual history. Bharatanatyam is also popular in other parts of South India, such as Andhra Pradesh, Karnataka, and Kerala, and is now performed by dancers of all backgrounds around the world.

"Indian classical dance is a reflection of the ancient wisdom of the country."

ജ

IV

Kathak: The Dance of North India

Kathak is a classical dance form that originated in northern India. It is one of the eight classical dance forms of India and has a rich cultural and spiritual history. The dance is characterized by its fast-paced footwork, intricate rhythms, and the use of hand gestures, or mudras, to convey different emotions and ideas.

Kathak has its roots in the Bhakti movement, a spiritual movement that emphasized devotion to God through music and dance. The dance form was originally performed by wandering minstrels, known as Kathakars, who would tell stories and convey moral messages through their dance performances. Over time, Kathak evolved to become a more formal dance style, incorporating elements of classical Indian dance and music.

The dance is known for its fast-paced footwork and

intricate rhythms. Dancers use a variety of steps and movements to create a dynamic and fluid performance. Kathak also incorporates elements of acting and storytelling, making it a complete form of expression. The dancers use their expressive eyes and facial expressions to convey different emotions and ideas.

Kathak is traditionally divided into two main styles: the Lucknow and Jaipur gharanas. The Lucknow gharana is known for its fluid and graceful movements, while the Jaipur gharana is known for its precise and sharp movements.

Kathak is not limited to North India alone, it is also popular in other parts of India such as Rajasthan, Gujarat and Maharashtra. These regions have their own unique styles of Kathak, which have been influenced by the local culture and traditions.

In recent years, Kathak has gained popularity around the world, and is now performed by dancers of all backgrounds. It is considered as a powerful medium for self-expression and has been used to raise awareness about important social and political issues.

In conclusion, Kathak is a classical dance form that originated in northern India. It is characterized by its fast-paced footwork, intricate rhythms, and the use of hand gestures, or mudras, to convey different emotions and ideas. The dance is rooted in the Bhakti movement, which emphasized devotion to God through music and dance, and it has evolved over time to become a more formal dance style incorporating elements of classical Indian dance and music. Kathak is also popular in other parts of India such as Rajasthan, Gujarat and Maharashtra, and is now performed by dancers of all backgrounds around the world.

"Indian dance is a form of storytelling, each movement painting a picture and conveying a message."

ꕥ

V

Kathakali: The Dance-Drama of Kerala

Kathakali is a classical dance-drama form that originated in the southern state of Kerala, India. It is one of the oldest and most distinctive forms of Indian classical dance and is known for its elaborate costumes, makeup, and facial expressions. The dance is characterized by its use of hand gestures, or mudras, and facial expressions to convey different emotions and ideas.

Kathakali has its roots in the traditional temple performances of Kerala, which were known as Kathakaliyattam. These performances were based on stories from Hindu mythology and were performed as part of temple rituals and ceremonies. Over time, Kathakali evolved to become a more formal dance-drama form, incorporating elements of classical Indian dance, music, and theater.

The dance-drama is known for its elaborate costumes, makeup, and facial expressions. The dancers use a variety of hand gestures and facial expressions to convey different emotions and ideas. The makeup, known as Chutti, is an important aspect of the performance and is used to create different characters and convey different emotions.

Kathakali performances typically last for several hours and often tell stories from Hindu mythology such as the Ramayana and the Mahabharata. The performances are usually accompanied by a live orchestra, which includes instruments such as the mridangam, chenda, and ganjira.

In recent years, Kathakali has gained popularity around the world, and is now performed by dancers of all backgrounds. It is considered as a powerful medium for self-expression and has been used to raise awareness about important social and political issues.

Kathakali is a classical dance-drama form that originated in the southern state of Kerala, India. It is known for its elaborate costumes, makeup, and facial expressions, as well as its use of hand gestures and facial expressions to convey different emotions and ideas. The dance-drama is rooted in the traditional temple performances of Kerala and is based on stories from Hindu mythology. Kathakali performances typically last for several hours and are accompanied by a live orchestra. In recent years, it has gained popularity around the world and is now performed by dancers of all backgrounds.

"Indian classical dance is the embodiment of grace and beauty."

VI

Kuchipudi: The Dance of Andhra Pradesh

Kuchipudi is a classical dance form that originated in the southern state of Andhra Pradesh, India. It is one of the eight classical dance forms of India and is characterized by its fluid movements and elegant footwork. The dance is known for its use of hand gestures, or mudras, to convey different emotions and ideas.

Kuchipudi has its origins in the traditional temple performances of Andhra Pradesh, which were known as Kuchipudi Yakshaganam. These performances were based on stories from Hindu mythology and were performed as part of temple rituals and ceremonies. Over time, Kuchipudi evolved to become a more formal dance form, incorporating elements of classical Indian dance, music, and theater.

The dance is known for its fluid movements and elegant footwork. Dancers use a variety of steps and movements to create a dynamic and fluid performance. Kuchipudi also incorporates elements of acting and storytelling, making it a complete form of expression. The dancers use their expressive eyes and facial expressions to convey different emotions and ideas.

Kuchipudi performances often tell stories through dance, using gestures and facial expressions to convey different emotions and ideas. The performances are usually accompanied by live music, which includes instruments such as the mridangam, veena, and flute.

In recent years, Kuchipudi has gained popularity around the world, and is now performed by dancers of all backgrounds. It is considered as a powerful medium for self-expression and has been used to raise awareness about important social and political issues.

Kuchipudi is a classical dance form that originated in the southern state of Andhra Pradesh, India. It is characterized by its fluid movements and elegant footwork, as well as its use of hand gestures, or mudras, to convey different emotions and ideas. The dance is rooted in the traditional temple performances of Andhra Pradesh and has evolved to become a more formal dance form, incorporating elements of classical Indian dance, music, and theater. Kuchipudi performances often tell stories through dance and are usually accompanied by live music. In recent years, it has gained popularity around the world and is now performed by dancers of all backgrounds.

"The fluid movements of Indian dance bring to life the poetry of the soul."

VII

Mohiniyattam: The Dance of Kerala

Mohiniyattam is a classical dance form that originated in the southern state of Kerala, India. It is a solo dance performed by women and is characterized by its graceful and fluid movements. The dance is known for its use of hand gestures, or mudras, to convey different emotions and ideas.

Mohiniyattam has its roots in the traditional temple performances of Kerala, which were known as Mohiniyattam. These performances were based on stories from Hindu mythology and were performed as part of temple rituals and ceremonies. Over time, Mohiniyattam evolved to become a more formal dance form, incorporating elements of classical Indian dance, music, and theater.

The dance is known for its graceful and fluid movements.

Dancers use a variety of steps and movements to create a dynamic and fluid performance. Mohiniyattam also incorporates elements of acting and storytelling, making it a complete form of expression. The dancers use their expressive eyes and facial expressions to convey different emotions and ideas.

Mohiniyattam performances often tell stories through dance, using gestures and facial expressions to convey different emotions and ideas. The performances are usually accompanied by live music, which includes instruments such as the mridangam, veena, and flute.

In recent years, Mohiniyattam has gained popularity around the world, and is now performed by dancers of all backgrounds. It is considered as a powerful medium for self-expression and has been used to raise awareness about important social and political issues.

Mohiniyattam is a classical dance form that originated in the southern state of Kerala, India. It is a solo dance performed by women and is characterized by its graceful and fluid movements. The dance is known for its use of hand gestures, or mudras, to convey different emotions and ideas. Mohiniyattam has its roots in the traditional temple performances of Kerala and has evolved to become a more formal dance form, incorporating elements of classical Indian dance, music, and theater. The performances often tell stories through dance, and are usually accompanied by live music. In recent years, it has gained popularity around the world and is now performed by dancers of all backgrounds.

"Indian dance is a medium of self-expression, a way to communicate emotions through movement."

ꕥ

VIII

Odissi: The Dance of Odisha

Odissi is a classical dance form that originated in the eastern state of Odisha, India. It is one of the eight classical dance forms of India and is characterized by its fluid movements and use of hand gestures, or mudras, to convey different emotions and ideas. The dance is known for its sensuous and expressive style, and its use of the tribhanga (triple bend) posture.

Odissi has its roots in the traditional temple performances of Odisha, which were known as Odra-Magadhi. These performances were based on stories from Hindu mythology and were performed as part of temple rituals and ceremonies. Over time, Odissi evolved to become a more formal dance form, incorporating elements of classical Indian dance, music, and theater.

The dance is known for its fluid movements and use of

hand gestures. Dancers use a variety of steps and movements to create a dynamic and fluid performance. Odissi also incorporates elements of acting and storytelling, making it a complete form of expression. The dancers use their expressive eyes and facial expressions to convey different emotions and ideas.

Odissi performances often tell stories from Hindu mythology, such as the stories of Lord Krishna, using gestures and facial expressions to convey different emotions and ideas. The performances are usually accompanied by live music, which includes instruments such as the pakhawaj, mardal, and sitar.

In recent years, Odissi has gained popularity around the world, and is now performed by dancers of all backgrounds. It is considered as a powerful medium for self-expression and has been used to raise awareness about important social and political issues.

Odissi is a classical dance form that originated in the eastern state of Odisha, India. It is characterized by its fluid movements and use of hand gestures, or mudras, to convey different emotions and ideas. The dance is known for its sensuous and expressive style, and its use of the tribhanga posture. Odissi has its roots in the traditional temple performances of Odisha and has evolved to become a more formal dance form, incorporating elements of classical Indian dance, music, and theater.

The performances often tell stories from Hindu mythology and are usually accompanied by live music. In recent years, it has gained popularity around the world and is now performed by dancers of all backgrounds. It is considered as a powerful medium for self-expression and has been used to raise awareness about important social and political issues. Additionally, the dance form has a strong connection to the temple and the religious practices of Odisha, the dance is often performed in temples as a form of worship and devotion to the gods. The dance form is a significant part of the cultural heritage of Odisha and continues to be an important aspect of the state's identity.

"The intricate choreography of Indian dance is a testament to the skill and dedication of the dancers."

ꕥ

IX

The Folk Dances of India

In addition to the classical dance forms, India also has a rich tradition of folk dances. Folk dances are an integral part of the rural culture and are performed to celebrate festivals, ceremonies, and other important events. Each state in India has its own unique folk dances, which reflect the local culture, traditions, and customs. Some of the most well-known folk dances of India include Bhangra, Dandiya, Garba, and Lavani.

Bhangra is a popular folk dance from the state of Punjab. It is usually performed during the harvest festival of Vaisakhi and is known for its energetic and lively moves. The dance is performed to the beat of dhol, a type of drum, and is characterized by its use of vigorous footwork and leaps.

Dandiya is a folk dance from the state of Gujarat. It is usually performed during the Navaratri festival and is known for its colorful and vibrant costumes. The dance is performed to the beat of dhol and is characterized by its use of sticks, which are struck together in rhythm.

Garba is another folk dance from the state of Gujarat. It is usually performed during the Navaratri festival and is known for its intricate footwork and use of colorful costumes. The dance is performed to the beat of dhol and is characterized by its circular movements, which symbolize the cycle of life.

Lavani is a popular folk dance from the state of Maharashtra. It is usually performed by women and is known for its sensuous and expressive style. The dance is performed to the accompaniment of a traditional musical ensemble, which includes instruments such as the dholki, a type of drum, and is characterized by its use of fast footwork and intricate body movements. The lyrics of the songs usually deal with social issues and everyday life.

These are just a few examples of the many folk dances that can be found in India. Each state has its unique traditional dances that reflect the local culture, traditions, and customs. Folk dances are an important part of India's cultural heritage and continue to be an important aspect of the country's identity. They are performed not only in rural areas but also in urban centers and on stages around the world, keeping alive the cultural legacy of India.

"In Indian dance, the body becomes a canvas for the artist's imagination."

☙

X

The Religious and Ritual Dances of India

In addition to classical and folk dances, India also has a rich tradition of religious and ritual dances. These dances are an integral part of the religious practices in India and are performed to honor the gods and goddesses, and to seek their blessings. These dances are performed in temples, shrines, and other sacred places, and are often accompanied by devotional music and singing.

One of the most well-known religious and ritual dances in India is the Bhangra, which is a traditional dance performed in the state of Punjab, during the festival of Baisakhi, to celebrate the harvest season. It is performed in front of the village shrine and the dancers offer the first fruits of the harvest to the deity.

Another famous religious dance is the Garba which is performed in the state of Gujarat during the Navaratri festival in honor of the goddess Durga. It is a circular dance, performed by women in colorful traditional attire, accompanied by music and singing. The dance is performed around an earthen lamp or an image of the goddess, symbolizing the victory of good over evil.

The traditional dance "Theyyam" is a ritual dance form of Kerala, performed in front of the village shrine. It is performed by men dressed in elaborate costumes, headgear and body paint, enacting the stories of gods and goddesses. It is considered as a medium of communication between the human and the divine.

The Chhau dance, which originated in the eastern states of West Bengal, Jharkhand and Odisha, is a traditional martial dance performed during the festival of Sohrai, to honor the god of agriculture and fertility. It is performed by men, dressed in traditional costumes, masks, and headgear, and is known for its acrobatic movements and use of weapons.

India has a rich tradition of religious and ritual dances which are an integral part of the religious practices in India. These dances are performed to honor the gods and goddesses and to seek their blessings. They are performed in temples, shrines, and other sacred places, and are often accompanied by devotional music and singing. Examples of these dances include Bhangra, Garba, Theyyam and Chhau, each one with its own unique style, costumes, and meaning, reflecting the local culture and customs, preserving the religious and spiritual heritage of India.

"Indian dance is a celebration of life, a tribute to the beauty of existence."

ജ

XI

The Impact of Indian classical Dance on the Modern World

Indian classical dance has had a significant impact on the modern world in terms of its cultural, artistic, and spiritual significance. The dance forms, which have evolved over centuries, have been passed down from generation to generation and continue to be performed and appreciated in India and around the world.

One of the most notable impacts of Indian classical dance on the modern world is the way it has influenced other dance forms and styles. Many Western dance forms, such as ballet and contemporary dance, have been influenced by the fluid movements and expressive gestures of Indian classical dance. Similarly, Indian classical dance has also been influenced by Western dance forms, resulting in a fusion of styles that has led to the development of new and unique dance forms.

Indian classical dance has also had a significant impact on the world of theater and film. Many plays, musicals, and films have incorporated elements of Indian classical dance into their performances, bringing a new dimension to the art of storytelling.

Another notable impact of Indian classical dance on the modern world is its ability to promote cross-cultural understanding and appreciation. As Indian classical dance is performed around the world, it has become a powerful tool for promoting cultural exchange and understanding. It allows audiences to experience and appreciate the rich cultural heritage of India, as well as the artistic and spiritual aspects of the dance form.

Indian classical dance has also been used as a medium for self-expression and social change. Many dancers have used the dance form to raise awareness about important social and political issues, such as gender equality, environmental conservation, and human rights.

Indian classical dance has had a significant impact on the modern world in terms of its cultural, artistic, and spiritual significance. It has influenced other dance forms and styles, has been incorporated into the world of theater and film, promotes cross-cultural understanding and appreciation, and has been used as a medium for self-expression and social change. The preservation and continuation of these dance forms is important not only to keep the cultural heritage alive but also to spread the message of peace, harmony and understanding through the art of dance.

"Indian classical dance is the perfect fusion of form and emotion."

ꙮ

XII

Bollywood and Indian Pop Dance

Bollywood and Indian pop dance refer to the style of dance seen in Indian cinema and popular music. Bollywood, a term derived from the words "Bombay" (the former name of Mumbai) and "Hollywood," refers to the Hindi-language film industry based in Mumbai, India. Indian pop dance, on the other hand, refers to the style of dance seen in Indian pop music, which is heavily influenced by Western pop music.

Bollywood dance is known for its high energy, colorful costumes, and elaborate choreography. The dance style often incorporates elements of classical Indian dance, such as Kathak and Bharatanatyam, as well as Western dance styles like hip-hop, jazz, and salsa. Bollywood dance is characterized by its use of expressive hand and facial gestures, as well as its use of complex footwork and body movements.

Indian pop dance is heavily influenced by Western pop music and is characterized by its fast-paced and upbeat style. It often incorporates elements of hip-hop, jazz, and contemporary dance, and is known for its use of modern choreography and catchy music.

Both Bollywood and Indian pop dance have become increasingly popular around the world in recent years. They are often performed in dance competitions and festivals, as well as in Bollywood-themed dance classes and workshops.

Bollywood and Indian pop dance refer to the style of dance seen in Indian cinema and popular music. Bollywood dance is known for its high energy, colorful costumes, and elaborate choreography, while Indian pop dance is characterized by its fast-paced and upbeat style, heavily influenced by Western pop music. Both have become increasingly popular around the world and are often performed in dance competitions and festivals, as well as in Bollywood-themed dance classes and workshops.

"Indian dance is a bridge between the past and the present, connecting us to our cultural heritage."

ᘓ

XIII

The conservation and preservation of Indian Dance

The conservation and preservation of Indian dance is an important task that is necessary to ensure that these ancient and rich dance forms continue to be passed down from generation to generation. The preservation of Indian dance involves not only maintaining the traditional techniques and choreography but also keeping the cultural and spiritual significance of the dance form alive.

One way to preserve Indian dance is through documentation and research. This includes recording and studying the choreography, music, and costumes associated with each dance form. This documentation can be used to create archives and training materials for future generations of dancers.

Another way to preserve Indian dance is through performance and education. This includes organizing performances, workshops, and dance festivals to showcase the different dance forms. It also includes providing training and education to future generations of dancers through dance schools and universities.

Another important aspect of preserving Indian dance is to ensure that traditional techniques and choreography are passed down accurately from guru to shishya (teacher to student). This is done through the guru-shishya tradition where the guru imparts not only the technical aspects of the dance but also the cultural and spiritual significance of the dance form.

In addition, there are many organizations, both government and non-governmental, that are working towards the preservation of Indian dance. They conduct research, document traditional dance forms, and work towards the promotion and preservation of Indian dance.

The conservation and preservation of Indian dance is an important task that is necessary to ensure that these ancient and rich dance forms continue to be passed down from generation to generation. This can be achieved through documentation and research, performance and education, accurate transmission of traditional techniques and choreography, and through the efforts of various organizations working towards the preservation of Indian dance.

"The spiritual aspect of Indian dance elevates it beyond the realm of entertainment and into something transcendental."

ꕥ

XIV

The education and training of Indian Dance

The education and training of Indian dance is a rigorous process that typically begins at a young age. Many dancers in India begin their training under the guidance of a guru, or teacher, who is an expert in the specific dance form. The guru-shishya (teacher-student) tradition is an important aspect of Indian dance education, as the guru not only teaches the technical aspects of the dance but also imparts the cultural and spiritual significance of the dance form.

The training typically includes learning the basic steps and movements, as well as the hand gestures, or mudras, that are specific to the dance form. Dancers also learn the choreography for traditional pieces, as well as the history and cultural context of the dance.

In addition to training in the specific dance form, dancers also receive training in music, as Indian dance is often performed to live music. This includes learning to sing and play traditional instruments, such as the veena, sitar, and tabla.

As the dancers progress in their training, they begin to learn more advanced choreography and movements, as well as how to improvise and create their own choreography. They also learn how to express emotions and tell stories through their dance.

In addition to traditional training, many dancers also receive formal education in dance through universities and dance schools. This can include studying the history and theory of dance, as well as learning about different dance forms from around the world.

The education and training of Indian dance is a rigorous process that typically begins at a young age under the guidance of a guru. It includes learning the basic steps and movements, as well as the hand gestures, or mudras, that are specific to the dance form. Dancers also receive training in music and receive formal education in dance through universities and dance schools. The education and training of Indian dance not only focuses on the technical aspects of the dance but also imparts the cultural and spiritual significance of the dance form.

"Indian dance is not just a performance, but a sacred ritual."

ℵ

XV

The ongoing relevance and significance of Indian Dance.

Indian dance continues to be relevant and significant in the modern world for a variety of reasons. One of the main reasons is its cultural and spiritual significance. Indian dance forms have their roots in the ancient culture and spiritual practices of India and continue to be an important aspect of the country's identity. They provide a connection to the country's rich history and heritage and help to preserve traditional customs and practices.

Another reason for the ongoing relevance and significance of Indian dance is its artistic value. Indian dance forms are known for their intricate choreography, fluid movements, and expressive gestures. They are a form of artistic expression that showcases the skill and talent of the dancers.

Indian dance also has a significant impact on the world of theater and film. Many plays, musicals, and films have incorporated elements of Indian classical dance into their performances, bringing a new dimension to the art of storytelling.

In addition, Indian dance promotes cross-cultural understanding and appreciation. As Indian dance is performed around the world, it allows audiences to experience and appreciate the rich cultural heritage of India, as well as the artistic and spiritual aspects of the dance form.

Indian dance has also been used as a medium for self-expression and social change. Many dancers have used the dance form to raise awareness about important social and political issues, such as gender equality, environmental conservation, and human rights.

Finally, Indian dance is an important part of the education and personal development of young people. It teaches discipline, focus, and dedication, and it provides an outlet for self-expression and creativity.

Indian dance continues to be relevant and significant in the modern world because of its cultural and spiritual significance, artistic value, impact on theater and film, ability to promote cross-cultural understanding, use as a medium for self-expression and social change and as an important part of the education and personal development of young people.

OTHER BOOKS OF THE AUTHOR

1. The Moments When I Met God
2. Kashiyile Theertha Pathangal
3. GURU GYAN VANI
4. Abhiprerak Gita
5. ASSI SE JAIN GHAT TAK
6. Hopelessness of Arjuna
7. The Soul and It's True Nature
8. Sense of Action (Karma)
9. Action through Wisdom
10. Action through Wisdom
11. THEORY AND PRACTICAL OF EVERY ACTION
12. LOGICAL UNDERSTANDING OF THE SUPREME
13. THE IMPERISHABLE SUPREME
14. Yatra Nishadraj se Hanuman Ghat Tak
15. Yatra Karnatak Ghat se Raja Ghat Tak
16. Yatra Pandey Ghat se Prayagraj Ghat Tak
17. Yatra Ranjendra Prasad Ghat se Dattatreya Ghat Tak
18. YaatraSindhiya Ghat se Gwaliar Ghat Tak
19. Yatra Mangala Gauri Ghat se Hanuman Gadhi Ghat Tak
20. Yatra Gaay Ghat Se Nishad Ghat Tak
21. MAA GANGA, GHATEN EVM UTSAV
22. Ganga Arti Dev Deepavali evam Any Utsav
23. Potentials of Digitalized India
24. VEDIC CONSCIOUSNESS
25. A Brief Introduction to Vedic Science
26. Kashi ke Barah Jyotirling
27. IMPACT OF MOTIVATION
28. Let's have a Milky Way Journey
29. Color Therapy in a Nutshell

30. Rigveda in a Nutshell
31. Yajurveda in a Nutshell
32. Samveda in a Nutshell
33. Atharva Veda in a Nutshell
34. Ayushman Bhava - Ayurveda
35. Srimad Bhagavad Gita and Upanishad Connection
36. Srimad Bhagavad Gita - an attempt to summarize each chapter.
37. Facts and Impact of Nakshatra
38. Astro Gems - NAVARATNA
39. Ekadashi - A Concise Overview
40. A Concise View of Hanuman Chalisa
41. Inspirational Gita
42. Nakshatraranyam
43. Summary of 18 Mahapuranas
44. Synopsis of 18 Upa Puranas
45. Rigvediya Upanishads
46. Shukla Yajurvediya Upanishads
47. Krishna Yajurvediya Upanishads
48. Samavediya Upanishads
49. Atharvavediya Upanishads
50. The Seven Great Sages
51. From Rocket Scientist to President Dr. APJ Abdul Kalam
52. The Visionary's Voice - Quotes of Dr. APJ Abdul Kalam
53. The Wisdom of Swami Vivekananda: Insights and Inspiration from a Legendary Spiritual Teacher
54. Ayurvedic Remedies from the Garden
55. Sages and Seers
56. Rising Strong – Motivational Stories of Women
57. Beyond Flames -Mystery stories of Funeral Ghat Manikarnika
58. The Origins of Tulsi: A Look at the Mythological Roots of the Plant"

59. The Holistic Cow: A Look at the Physical, Spiritual, and Cultural Importance of Cows in India
60. Arts of Healing
61. Exploring the Divine
62. Understanding Five Elements
63. The Etymology of Ram
64. Symbols of India
65. Voice of Change (About Speeches of Great Men)
66. She Speaks (About Speeches of Great Women)
67. Patriotism on Celluloid – Brief About Patriotic Films
68. The Music of Motivation: A Brief Guide to Inspirational Film Songs
69. Unlocking the Secrets of the Dashopanishads
70. A Cultural Mosaic
71. Ancient Traditions, Modern Minds
72. Ecos of Ancient Wisdom
73. Beneath the Surface
74. From Temples to Ashrams
75. Sages of the Subcontinent
76. The Art of Healling (Ayurveda, Yoga & Naturopathy)
77. Indian Kitchen
78. The Festivals of India
79. The Indian Epics Retold
80. The Power of Mantras
81. The Indian River Ganges
82. The Indian Architecture
83. Rites of Passage
84. The Indian Silk Road
85. The Indian Literature
86. The Indian Villages
87. The Indian Folks & Crafts
88. The Way of Buddha
89. The Ramayan of Tulsidas

90. Astrological Remedies
91. The Secret Power of Motivation
92. Secret of Developing your Inner Strength

Contact

DR. JAGADEESH PILLAI

PhD in Vedic Science

Four Times Guinness World Record Holder

Winner of Mahatma Gandhi Vishwa Shanti Puraskar and Global Peace Ambassador

Gemology, Astro & Vastu Consultant - Spiritual Counselor

Consultant for designing World Record Ideas

Efficient Tarot Card Reader

9839093003

myrichindia@gmail.com

drjagadeeshpillai@facebook

drjagadeeshpillai@instagram

jagadeeshpillai@youtube

www. JAGADEESHPILLAI.com

|| LOKAHA SAMASTHAHA SUKHINO BHAVANTU ||

Printed by Libri Plureos GmbH in Hamburg,
Germany